T0058042

# WARHORSES

# WARHORSES

POEMS

## YUSEF KOMUNYAKAA

FARRAR, STRAUS AND GIROUX

*New York*

FARRAR, STRAUS AND GIROUX
18 West 18th Street, New York 10011

Printed in the United States of America
Published in 2008 by Farrar, Straus and Giroux
First paperback edition, 2009

Grateful acknowledgment is made to the following publications, in which some of these poems originally appeared: *The American Poetry Review* (an excerpt of "Autobiography of My Alter Ego," which received the Jerome J. Shestack Poetry Prize in 2007); *Mandorla*; *Mantis*; *The Nation*; *The New Yorker*; *Ploughshares*; *Poetry*; *Rattle*; and *Washington Square*. Excerpts from "Love in the Time of War" and "Autobiography of My Alter Ego" appeared in *Totem*, a book translated into Italian by Antonella Francini and published by Casa Editrice Le Lettere. Some of the sections of "Love in the Time of War" were first collected in a fine press book under the same title, published by Robin Price.

The Library of Congress has cataloged the hardcover edition as follows:
Komunyakaa, Yusef.
     Warhorses / Yusef Komunyakaa.— 1st ed.
        p.    cm.
     Poems reflecting on love and war.

     PS3561.O455W37 2008
     811'.54—dc22

                                                                2007051760

Paperback ISBN: 978-0-374-53191-1

Designed by Gretchen Achilles

www.fsgbooks.com

P1

TO KASIA AND MY FRIENDS

# CONTENTS

LOVE IN THE TIME OF WAR                                      1

"The jawbone of an ass. A shank"                            3

"Gilgamesh's Humbaba was a distant drum"                    4

"Here, the old masters of Shock & Awe"                      5

"The Mameluke—slave & warrior—springs"                      6

"They swarmed down over the town"                           7

"My wide hips raised two warriors"                          8

"Hand-to-hand: the two hugged each other"                   9

"Tribe. Clan. Valley & riverbank.
  Country. Continent. Interstellar"                          10

"The drummer's hands were bloody."                          11

"Tonight, the old hard work of love"                        12

"When our hands caress bullets & grenades"                  13

"A bottle-nosed dolphin swims midnight water"               14

"Someone's beating a prisoner."                             15

"His name is called. A son's lost voice"                    16


HEAVY METAL                                                 17

The Helmet                                                  19

The Catapult                                                20

Warhorses                                                   21

The Clay Army                                               26

The Panorama     28

Guernica     30

Grenade     32

The Towers     33

Heavy Metal Soliloquy     34

The Warlord's Garden     35

Surge     37

Clouds     38

The Hague     39

The Devil Comes on Horseback     41

The Crying Hill     42

AUTOBIOGRAPHY OF MY ALTER EGO     43

The jawbone of an ass. A shank
braided with shark teeth. A garrote.
A shepherd's sling. A jagged stone
that catches light & makes warriors
dance to a bull-roarer's lamentation.
An obsidian ax. A lion-skin drum
& reed flute. A nightlong prayer
to gods stopped at the mouth of a cave.

The warrior-king summons one goddess
after another to his bloodstained pallet.
If these dear ones live inside his head
they still dress his wounds with balms
& sacred leaves, & kiss him
back to strength, back to a boy.

Gilgamesh's Humbaba was a distant drum
pulsing among the trees, a slave to the gods,
a foreign tongue guarding the sacred cedars
down to a pale grubworm in the tower
before Babel. Invisible & otherworldly,
he was naked in the king's heart,
& his cry turned flies into maggots
& blood reddened the singing leaves.

When Gilgamesh said Shiduri, a foreplay
of light was on the statues going to the river
between them & the blinding underworld.
She cleansed his wounds & bandaged his eyes
at the edge of reason, & made him forget
birthright, the virgins in their bridal beds.

Here, the old masters of Shock & Awe
huddle in the war room, talking iron,
fire & sand, alloy & nomenclature.
Their hearts lag against the bowstring
as they daydream of Odysseus's bed.
But to shoot an arrow through the bull's-eye
of twelve axes lined up in a row
is to sleep with one's eyes open. Yes,

of course, there stands lovely Penelope
like a trophy, still holding the brass key
against her breast. How did the evening star
fall into that room? Lost between plot
& loot, the plucked string turns into a lyre
humming praises & curses to the unborn.

The Mameluke—slave & warrior—springs
out of dust & chance, astride his horse
at sunrise, one with its rage & gallop,
wedded to its flanks & the sound of hooves
striking clay & stone, carried into the sway
of desert grass. His double-edged saber
bloodies valleys & hills, a mirage,
till he arrives at a gate of truth in myth:
for a woman to conceive in this place & time,
she must be in the arms of a warrior riding
down through the bloody ages,
over bones of the enemy in the sand
& along the river in a sultan's dream,
till their child is born on horseback.

They swarmed down over the town
& left bodies floating in the ditches
& moats. Bloated with silence,
blue with flies on the rooftops.

They gave the children candy
made of honey & nuts, scented with belladonna
to weed out the weak. Bundles of silk
rolled out like a rainbow for the women.

On the wild forgetful straw beds
they created a race, a new tongue
to sing occidental prayers & regrets.

Their camphor lanterns mastered darkness.
All the taboos of lovemaking were broken.
Soon, laughter rose again from the fields.

My wide hips raised two warriors
from sweat & clay, blood sonata
& birth cry. I said anger & avarice,
& they called themselves Cain & Abel.
I said gold, & they opened up the earth.
I said love, & they ventured east
& west, south & north. I said evil,
& they lost themselves in reflected rivers.

After scrimmages across Asia Minor
& guarding kingly ransom in the Horn of Africa,
my sons journeyed home to peasant bread
& salt meat, to whorish doubts & wonder,
but when I flung my arms open at the threshold
they came to me as unseasoned boys.

Hand-to-hand: the two hugged each other
into a naked tussle, one riding the other's back,
locked in a double embrace. One
forced the other to kiss the ground,

as he cursed & bit into an earlobe.
They shook beads of dew off the grass.
One worked his fingers into the black soil,
& could feel a wing easing out of his scapula.

That night, the lucky one who gripped
a stone like Mercury weighing the planet
in his palm, who knew windfall & downfall,

he fell against his sweetheart again
& again, as if holding that warrior in his arms,
& couldn't stop himself from rising off the earth.

Tribe. Clan. Valley & riverbank. Country. Continent. Interstellar
aborigines. Squad. Platoon. Company. Battalion. Regiment. Hive
& swarm. Colony. Legend. Laws. Ordinances. Statutes. Grid
coordinates. Maps. Longitude. Latitude. Property lines drawn
in unconsecrated dust. Sextant & compass. Ledger. Loyalty
oath. Therefore. Hereinbefore. Esprit de corps. Lock & load.
Bull's-eye. Maggie's drawers. Little Boy. Fat Man. Circle
in the eye. Bayonet. Skull & Bone. Them. Body count. Thou

& I. Us. Honey. Darling. Sweetheart, was I talking war in my sleep
again? Come closer. Yes, place your head against my chest.
The moon on a windowsill. I want to stitch up all your wounds
with kisses, but I also know that sometimes the seed is hurting
for red in the soil. Sometimes. Sometimes I hold you like Achilles'
shield, your mouth on mine, my trembling inside your heart & sex.

The drummer's hands were bloody.
The players of billowy bagpipes
marched straight into the unblinking
muzzle flash. The fife player
conjured a way to disappear
inside himself: The bullets zinged
overhead & raised dust devils
around his feet. He crossed a river.

Bloodstained reeds quivered in the dark.
He rounded a hedgerow thick with blooms
& thorns. Some lone, nameless bird
fell in tune with his fife, somewhere
in the future, & he saw a blue nightgown
fall to the floor of an eye-lit room.

Tonight, the old hard work of love
has given up. I can't unbutton promises
or sing secrets into your left ear
tuned to quivering plucked strings.

No, please. I can't face the reflection
of metal on your skin & in your eyes,
can't risk weaving new breath into war fog.
The anger of the trees is rooted in the soil.

Let me drink in your newly found river
of sighs, your way with incantations.
Let me see if I can't string this guitar

& take down your effigy of moonlight
from the cross, the dogwood in bloom
printed on memory's see-through cloth.

When our hands caress bullets & grenades,
or linger on the turrets & luminous wings
of reconnaissance planes, we leave glimpses
of ourselves on the polished hardness.
We surrender skin, hair, sweat, & fingerprints.
The assembly lines hum to our touch,
& the grinding wheels record our laments
& laughter into the bright metal.

I touch your face, your breasts, the flower
holding a world in focus. We give ourselves
to each other, letting the workday slide
away. Afterwards, lying there facing the sky,
I touch the crescent-shaped war wound. Yes,
the oldest prayer is still in my fingertips.

A bottle-nosed dolphin swims midnight water
with plastic explosives strapped to her body.
A black clock ticks in her half-lit brain.
Brighter than some water-headed boy
in a dream, she calls from the depths. The voice
of her trainer, a Navy Seal, becomes a radio wave
guiding her to the target. One eye is asleep
& the other is the bright side of the moon.

The trainer & his wife sway to the rise & fall
of their water bed, locked in each other's arms.
They're taken down into a breathless country
where Neptune wrestles the first & last siren,
to where a shadow from that other world
torpedoes along like a fat, long bullet.

Someone's beating a prisoner.
Someone's counting red leaves
falling outside a clouded window
in a secret country. Someone
holds back a river, but the next rabbit jab
makes him piss on the stone floor.
The interrogator orders the man
to dig his grave with a teaspoon.

The one he loves, her name
died last night on his tongue.
To revive it, to take his mind off
the electric wire, he almost said,
There's a parrot in a blue house
that knows the password, a woman's name.

His name is called. A son's lost voice
hovers near a fishing hole in August.
His name is called. A lover's hand
disturbs a breath of summer cloth.
His name is called a third time,
but his propped-up boots & helmet
refuse to answer. The photo remains silent,
& his name hangs in the high rafters.

She tenderly hugs the pillow,
whispering his name. The dog
rises beside the bedroom door
& wanders to the front door,
& stands with its head cocked,
listening for a name in a dead language.

HEAVY
METAL

# THE HELMET

Perhaps someone was watching
a mud turtle or an armadillo
skulk along an old interminable footpath,
armored against sworn enemies,
& then that someone shaped a model,
nothing but the mock-up of a hunch
into a halved, rounded, carved-out
globe of wood covered with animal skin.
How many battles were fought before
bronze meant shield & breastplate,
before iron was fired, hammered, & taught
to outwit the brain's glacial weather,
to hold an edge? God-inspired,
it was made to deflect a blow
or blade, to make the light pivot
on the battlefield. Did the soldiers
first question this new piece of equipment,
did they laugh like a squad of Hells Angels,
saying, Is this our ration bowl for bonemeal,
& gore? The commander's sunrise
was stolen from the Old Masters,
& his coat of arms made the shadows
kneel. The ram, the lion, the ox,
the goat—folkloric. Horse-headed
helmets skirted the towering cedars
till only a lone vulture circled the sky
as first & last decipher of the world.

# THE CATAPULT

At first,
warriors crawled into the ditch
with the demon
& wrestled the contraption
down to grapple & clutch,
as if cinching a stormy sail
on the high seas
or tussling a bull
on a cliff ledge. Loaded
with taut & release—timbers & braided hide, hemp
wound into a groan tied down on a rack,
a bowstring pulled by Zeus—
the stone nestled, ready to lift
& soar to its bull's-eye.
Exhausted by tug & sway, held there
by the great slingshot,
warriors bowed at the foot
of the cross.

# WARHORSES

*A performance piece for voices, musicians, & dancers.*
*Two or three seesaws are on the stage.*


Half horse
       & half man—
   Hercules wrestled himself
out of a block of marble,
   as rider & slayer, one
rooted within the other—
gravity & exultation. Half
      earth & half reason,
all astonishment & heft,
   the centaur whinnied
& rose out of stone, born
   begging to be lassoed
       & driven back
to the silence of stone.


◎


Before stone
   was again allowed to breathe,
a goddess's fingers tapped
Pegasus's clavicle
till wings splayed.

She was counting
each bone, counting
as if divining a harp.
Is this an idea of a horse
before there were horses,
before the gods of the horse
flew down from the hills?

◎

At first, their backs
    were too weak
to carry a man, but over innumerable years
    the horse people
rode steeds bareback across the steppe.
    War was in the tundra. It was in the blood
when the Scourge of God crested a hilltop
    astride a spotted mare, galloping with the sun
on his shoulder, Orion in his head.
    The infamous dead trailed behind
& burning huts smoldered at twilight,
    his relay horses eating the grass
down to naked stubble & pith.

◎

When Cortés & his men rode
through the virginal grasses
& man-high ferns, they came as gods
out of a dream, man & horse
one & the same blood, holding up a cross
& a sword, saying to the Aztecs,
Which one do you believe in?
Montezuma, if you do not show us
the gold, there is no earthly sacrifice
that can save your heart from the crows.

◎

Horses carried men to reed boats.
Horses carried the Lion-hearted
& Jackal-headed, as they prayed
they'd find crosses ahead, in the fog.
Horses carried men to the quartering.
Horses carried men to grasslands
of the Crow, Shawnee, & Apache.
Horses carried men to the gangplank.
Horses carried men to Shangri-la,
Nebo, San Juan Hill, & Xanadu.
Horses carried men to the trenches
stinking of mustard gas & betrayal.
Horses carried men to the hanging trees.
Horses carried men to the Angel of Mons
sleeping in a snow-covered minefield.

◎

War-broken & torn down
    to nothing
but stripped muscles
    & tendons, to dreams of the past,
she was now at ease
    with the sky
sliding across her back,
    the wild river running
along with her half-
    stumbling gait.
In her eyes, a horse nation
    gallops beside her—
Indian ponies & white stallions
    of generals. She's wind-swept
& heart-driven, grease lightning
    & laggard, corralled by the dead.

◎

Horsepower harnessed beneath a metal hood
whinnied & grunted in the brain,
& that was enough to master
longitude & latitude
in a single throttle.
A gallop
        in the mind—
a gallop
        in the body—
the whole world
rolling with breakneck
accelerated cognition
running on gas & oil

turning beneath hooves
echoing cave paintings
in a land of shadows.

◎

Beauty rides the one-eyed horse
    beyond adoration & blame,
into the blood's flow & tidal point,
    beyond the cadence & upsurge
of wind in the swept-back hair
    as a lioness would straddle
an antelope's back in a swish
    of high grass. Beauty rides
the one-eyed horse beyond the gate
    spiked with shards of glass,
into an undreamt vista of stardust
    & free will, facing the climate
out of which she has sprung,
    her body rising & singing
the speed of the green terraces.

# THE CLAY ARMY

When the roof of the First Emperor of Qin's tomb
caved in, six thousand life-size terra-cotta soldiers knelt

beneath its crumbling weight in the first pit,
alongside horses & chariots. Centuries before,

when the clay figures stood in perfect formation,
the rebel general Xiang Yu looted this sanctuary

of the dead, sequestering the bronze weapons
honed by these bodyguards of the afterworld

to kill the heirs of the charging drums & bells.
All their bright regimental colors are eaten away.

Their etched mouths are shaped for secret oaths.
Their eyes can see into the old lost seasons,

& their noses are dilated as if smelling lilies
in a valley. Rank is carved into each topknot,

tassel, & strand. The blind can read insignia
grooved into the uniforms. In the second pit,

in its L-shaped chamber, cavalrymen & horses
with pricked ears peer out of the red earth,

unbridled by time. Some warriors are sculpted
in unbroken *taijiquan* stances. In the third pit,

royal commanders huddle with scrimmages
in broken heads. The statues rise again in flanks

after they are pieced together & bandaged
with strips of wet clay. The last pit is empty,

no more than a cave, furnished with shadows
& imperial dreams from the Forbidden City.

# THE PANORAMA

It seems we've slowed down the spinning earth,
standing in this rotunda, holding each other's hand,

encircled by colors. But there's so much blood
up there I can't tell where the false terrain begins.

The peasants on the canvas wall, who are used to dust
in their spit, rose for their battle commander, swinging

long-handled scythes against the Russian infantrymen
& grenadiers, as if cutting wild fields of rye & rape.

The open-air light makes it hard to tell if the tall whitish
birches are real or painted. It took them only nine months

to perfect this motion of battle, its raw depth & upsweep,
the charge & clash, the horses in midstride, the paced-off

land captured. With picks & pikes, the smoke soldiers
pierce the living stronghold. Here's the Cossack gunner

trying to light the cannon fuse, & this is the day's hero
who stabs him with a scythe & flings his Krakow cap

over the gun's breach. Now two peasants pull the cannon
to their position with ropes. Our Lady of Czestochowa

unfurled in the wounded daylight. Dead horses beside
their dead riders. The supply columns & runaway carts—

the snapped harnesses—block the Hussar relief troops
as Polish sharpshooters take aim. We stand there

as if attacked from front & rear, from left & right,
cavaliers caught in a waterfall of hues, momentarily

silenced, & I can hear only a battlefield trumpet,
calling & calling, desperately calling.

# GUERNICA

Lightning struck. It left a courtyard of totems
on their backs or kneeling in the midday dusk,

& a German bomber rose among the clouds,
headed for another grid square on a map.

When cries of the burning city reached Picasso
in Paris, a woman's wailing was in his head,

but all the king's men—all the king's horsemen
couldn't mend this mirage of toppled statuary.

He mounted a tall stepladder to reach the top
of his canvas. Black & white, shades of gray—

days of splintered shadows & angry nights
writhed at the painter's feet. All the years

of exile bowed to him, & then time's ashes
drew past & present future perfectly together:

Although it was only a replica woven on a wall
at the UN, before the statesmen could speak

of war, they draped a blue cloth over the piece,
so cameras weren't distracted by the dead child

in her mother's embrace. The severed hand
grips a broken sword. The woman falling

through the floor of a burning house is still
falling. The horse screams a human voice.

The dumbstruck bull pines for the matador.
There's always a fallen warrior whispering

a stone's promise, waiting for a star,
his mouth agape.

# GRENADE

There's no rehearsal to turn flesh into dust so quickly. A hair trigger, a cocked hammer in the brain, a split second between a man & infamy. It lands on the ground—a few soldiers duck & the others are caught in a half-run—& one throws himself down on the grenade. All the watches stop. A flash. Smoke. Silence. The sound fills the whole day. Flesh & earth fall into the eyes & mouths of the men. A dream trapped in midair. They touch their legs & arms, their groins, ears, & noses, saying, What happened? Some are crying. Others are laughing. Some are almost dancing. Someone tries to put the dead man back together. "He just dove on the damn thing, sir!" A flash. Smoke. Silence. The day blown apart. For those who can walk away, what is their burden? Shreds of flesh & bloody rags gathered up & stuffed into a bag. Each breath belongs to him. Each song. Each curse. Every prayer is his. Your body doesn't belong to your mind & soul. Who are you? Do you remember the man left in the jungle? The others who owe their lives to this phantom, do they feel like you? Would his loved ones remember him if that little park or statue erected in his name didn't exist, & does it enlarge their lives? You wish he'd lie down in that closed coffin, & not wander the streets or enter your bedroom at midnight. The woman you love, she'll never understand. Who would? You remember what he used to say: "If you give a kite too much string, it'll break free." That unselfish certainty. But you can't remember when you began to live his unspoken dreams.

# THE TOWERS

Yes, dear son
dead, but not gone,
some were good, ordinary
people who loved a pinch of salt
on a slice of melon. Good,
everyday souls gazing up
at birds every now & then,
a flash of wings like blood
against the skylights. Well,
others were good as gold
certificates in a strongbox
buried in the good earth. Yes,
two or three stopped to give
the homeless vet on the corner
a shiny quarter or silver dime,
while others walked dead
into a fiery brisance, lost
in an eternity of Vermeer.
A few left questions blighting
the air. Does she love me?
How can I forgive him?
Why does the dog growl
when I turn the doorknob?
Some were writing e-mails
& embossed letters to ghosts
when the first plane struck.
The boom of one thousand
trap drums was thrown against
a metallic sky. A century of blue
vaults opened, & rescue workers
scrambled with their lifelines
down into the dark, sending up
plumes of disbelieving dust.
They tried to soothe torn earth,
to stretch skin back over the
pulse beat. When old doubts
& shame burn, do they smell
like anything we've known?
When happiness is caught off
guard, when it beats its wings
bloody against the bony cage,
does it die screaming or laughing?

No,
none,
not a single one
possessed wings as agile
& unabashedly decorous as yours,
son. Not even those lovers who
grabbed each other's hand & leapt
through the exploding windows.
Pieces of sky fell with the glass,
bricks, & charred mortar. Nothing
held together anymore. Machines
grunted & groaned into the heap
like gigantic dung beetles. After
planes had flown out of a scenario
in Hollywood, few now believed
their own feet touched the ground.
Signed deeds & promissory notes
floated over the tangled streets,
& some hobbled in broken shoes
toward the Brooklyn Bridge.
The cash registers stopped on
decimal points, in a cloud bank
of dead cell phones & dross.
Search dogs crawled into tombs
of burning silence. September
could hardly hold itself upright,
but no one donned any feathers.
Apollo was at Ground Zero
because he knows everything
about bandaging up wounds.
Men dug hands into quavering
flotsam, & they were blinded by
the moon's indifference. No,
Voice, I don't know anything
about infidels, though I can see
those men shaving their bodies
before facing a malicious god
in the mirror. The searchlights
throbbed. No, I'm not Daedalus,
but I've walked miles in a circle,
questioning your wings of beeswax
& crepe singed beyond belief.

# HEAVY METAL SOLILOQUY

After a nightlong white-hot hellfire
of blue steel, we rolled into Baghdad,
plugged into government-issued earphones,
hearing hard rock. The drum machines
& revved-up guitars roared in our heads.
All their gods were crawling on all fours.
These bloated replicas of horned beetles
drew us to targets, as if they could breathe
& think. The turrets rotated 360 degrees.
The infrared scopes could see through stone.
There were mounds of silver in the oily dark.
Our helmets were the only shape of the world.
Lightning was inside our titanium tanks,
& the music was almost holy, even if blood
was now leaking from our eardrums.
We were moving to a predestined score
as bodies slumped under the bright heft
& weight of thunderous falling sky.
Locked in, shielded off from desert sand
& equatorial eyes, I was inside a womb,
a carmine world, caught in a limbo,
my finger on the trigger, getting ready to die,
getting ready to be born.

# THE WARLORD'S GARDEN

He has bribed the thorns
to guard his poppies.
They intoxicate the valley
with their forbidden scent,
reddening the horizon
till it is almost as if
they aren't there.
Maybe the guns guard
only the notorious
dreams in his head.
The weather is kind
to every bloom,
& the fat greenish bulbs
form a galaxy of fantasies
& beautiful nightmares.
After they're harvested
& molded into kilo sacks
of malleable brown powder,
they cross the country
on horseback,
on river rafts
following some falling star,
& then ride men's shoulders
down to the underworld,
down to rigged scales
where money changers
& gunrunners linger
in the pistol-whipped hush
of broad daylight. No,
now, it shouldn't be long

before the needle's bright tip
holds a drop of woeful bliss,
before the fifth horseman of the Apocalypse
gallops again the night streets of Europe.

# SURGE

Always more. No, we aren't too ashamed to prod celestial beings
into our machines. Always more body bags & body counts for oath
   takers
& sharpshooters. Always more. More meat for the gibbous grinder
& midnight mover. There's always someone standing on a hill, half
   lost
behind dark aviation glasses, saying, If you asked me, buddy, you
   know,
it could always be worse. A lost arm & leg? Well, you could be stone
   dead.
Here comes another column of apparitions to dig a lifetime of
   roadside graves.
Listen to the wind beg. Always more young, strong, healthy bodies.
   Always.


Yes. What a beautiful golden sunset. (*A pause*) There's always that
   one naked soul
who'll stand up, shuffle his feet a little, & then look the auspicious,
   would-be gods
in the eyes & say, Enough! I won't give another good guess or black
   thumbnail
to this mad dream of yours! An ordinary man or woman. Alone. A
   mechanic
or cowboy. A baker. A farmer. A hard hat. A tool-&-die man.
   Almost a smile
at the corners of a mouth. A fisherman. A tree surgeon. A
   seamstress. Someone.

# CLOUDS

The plane bobs like a cork
in an air pocket, my heart
inside my belly, & then it levels out.
The woman seated beside me
is now almost in my arms.
She smiles & says, I'm sorry,
& then I see the boy soldiers
on the cover of the magazine
she's holding. Cloud-griffins
& cloud-horses pantomime the 747.

I see my face among their boyish poses
reflected in the airplane window,
& then I hear bloody tom-toms
in a deep valley, as my mind
runs along with an ancestor's,
three steps into a moonless interior
before he's captured & sold
for swatches of bright cloth
& a few glass beads. A spear dance
awakens the daydreamer's blue hour.

What tribal scrimmage centuries ago
brought me here to this moment
where Georgia O'Keeffe's clouds
are flat-white against an ocean, before
the plane touches down at La Guardia
this morning? The boy soldiers
huddle around someone shot
on the ground, the raised dust
coloring their faces, clothes,
& memory the pigment of dust.

# THE HAGUE

The dictator sits astride his throne
while an iridescent bluebottle
throbs against a windowpane
of the bathroom in his prison cell.

He has a globe that spins on a desk.
Countries appear. People disappear
overnight. He strains to touch
the upturned hourglass mirrored

on a sheet of bright stainless steel
welded to a wall, but only the dead
come to life in the glare. Tomorrow,
he'll speak to the authorities again

about the television watching him
like some one-eyed Cyclops
in a cave. Half-written letters
confess to his wife & sweetheart

unbearable desires. The moonlight
of polished knives & brass bullets
dances in his eyes. Just months ago
he'd crook a finger & call hundreds

to his side. Oh, yes, it's hard to forget
those kisses bought with a promise
of gold & diamonds. Blood money
is now less than dust on a damp leaf.

A brown spider sits, waiting on the edge
of a high window, as if it isn't there.

A speck of red glows on her egg sac.
Brightness is still the oldest warning.

In the old days, the general's ribbons
& medals rainbowed across his chest,
& if he were interrogating himself,
by now, blood would be on the walls.

# THE DEVIL COMES ON HORSEBACK

Although the sandy soil's already red,
the devil still comes on horseback
at midnight, with old obscenities
in his head, galloping along a pipeline
that ferries oil to the black tankers
headed for Shanghai. Traveling
through folklore & songs, prayers
& curses, he's a windmill of torches
& hot lead, rage & plunder, bloodlust
& self-hatred, rising out of the Seven Odes,
a Crow of the Arabs. Let them wing
& soar, let them stumble away on broken feet,
let them beg with words of the unborn,
let them strum a dusty oud of gut & gourd,
still the devil rides a shadow at daybreak.
Pity one who doesn't know his bloodline
is rape. He rides with a child's heart
in his hands, a head on a crooked staff,
& he can't stop charging the night sky
till his own dark face turns into ashes
riding a desert wind's mirage.

# THE CRYING HILL

Lately, I've stood between one self
& another self, trying to call across
the gone years, & my voice floats
from a tower of Babel, saying,
Yes, I need my arms around you
to anchor myself. Or, maybe I hear Ray
with the volume turned down, singing
     "If I were a mountain jack
             I'd call my baby back."
Or, I am hearing again that old man
facing a silent field of land mines,
circled by barbed wire, calling
his daughter's name over a loudspeaker
on his crying hill near the Golan Heights.
The sunlight glints off his eyeglasses.
She arrives like an apparition unbound
from a stone. Whenever he comes here,
he goes away with pocketsful of dirt.
He's lamenting her mother's ashes
given months ago to the Sea of Galilee
one sunset. What is she saying to him,
her head thrown back, her black hair
flowing around her? She has a bouquet
of red roses. But for a second, an eye
blink, he thought she'd been wounded.
Do the flowers mean a birth or death?
A whisper floats out of the loudspeaker.
He remembers when he was wild-hearted,
climbing these hills with his two friends,
Seth & Horus, both dead now for years.
They were kings, three laughing boys,
daring the small animals to speak.

You see these eyes?
                    You see this tongue?
You see these ears?
                    They may detect a quiver
in the grass, an octave
                    higher or lower—
a little different, an iota,
                    but they're no different
than your eyes & ears.
                    I can't say I don't know
how Lady Liberty's
                    tilted in my favor or yours,
that I don't hear what I hear
                    & don't see what I see
in the cocksure night
                    from Jefferson & Washington
to terrorists in hoods & sheets
                    in a black man's head.
As he feels what's happening
                    you can also see & hear
what's happening to him.
                    You see these hands?
They know enough to save us.
                    I'm trying to say this: True,
I'm a cover artist's son,
                    born to read between lines,
but I also know that you know
                    a whispered shadow in the trees
is the collective mind
                    of insects, birds, & animals
witnessing what we do to each other.

◎

My father was a cover artist
                        back in the late '40s, early '50s. So,
I grew up with Mister Bones
                        talking black & making love
to my mother in a midnight room.
                                He was debonair in powder blue
suits & paisley ascots, in patent leather
                        shoes that moved the sky
as he walked across the crabgrass.
                                When he wasn't on the road
or here at the Chimera Club
                        like a hawk at the cash drawer,
he lived in a room of mirrors,
                                his chrome Philco turntable
spinning up the bottom of a well
                        as he tried to capture
Nat Cole & Mister B.
                        The voice was always his
when he spoke, but I heard
                        the yardman's "Amazing Grace"
those nights & days he sang.

◎

Oh, so you don't know
                    what a cover artist is?
Well, let's say he was
                    someone like Pat Boone, Elvis,
or my father, when the radios
                    & jukeboxes were all red-lined.
Music. Sex. You know.
                    Back when they'd run a rope
down the middle of the dance floor
                    quick as running a flag
up a hundred-foot steel pole
                    or tossing a noose
over an oak limb
                    at the edge of a field—
a riot of red blooms at dusk.

◎

The first person I ever loved
                          was a tall black woman
named Roberta. Roberta Washington
                               was over six feet,
& she was my mother's salvation:
                               she cooked our meals, scrubbed
our floors, lit the candles
                          on the dining table, cleaned up
my shit & vomit, sang butterflies
                               & hummingbirds to the windows,
kissed me to sleep, washed & ironed,
                               comforted my mother
when my father was touring, lost
                          in his borrowed falsetto,
& to me she was also the captain
                               of all the ships on the sea
& all the planes in the sky.
                          Washington—there's a whole country
& tons of gunpowder
                          & broken vows sealed in that name.
Three or four times,
                     I remember Roberta undressing
down to her blue slip
                     in the August heat & pulling me into her lap,
the two of us sipping lemonade
                               as the blades of the black electric fan
spun us off to a distant land.
                          I lived in some other world,
some other time, & then one day
                               I fell deeply in love
with my mother's voice as she read

                        a story about lost treasures
on Blackbeard's island. A soft bell
                        tolled inside her voice.
But even now, if I close my eyes
                        & lean my head back
this way, I can almost remember—
                        I don't know if it's true—
I can almost remember
                        suckling Roberta's breasts,
& the idea trembles inside me.

◎

I remember
            when no one could coax me
to say a word,
            when I'd stand there
thinking about the man
                        in the moon, though words
filled my head.
            But one day Roberta
brought a puppy with her
                        & she said, She's yours
if you give her a name,
                        & I whispered into her ear
*Bullet*. My tongue
            was locked against the world.
When I tried to speak
            to my father, I spoke
someone else's voice.
                        My mother would take me
into her arms & rock me
                        to sleep. One day,
I picked up *Running*
            *Behind My Shadow*
& began to read to Bullet,
                        & I believe
I've been talking ever since.

◎

Summers when Mother & I visited
                    Tulsa, Grandpa Augustus
would say, Boy, you
                    were born one hundred steps
ahead of many. You
                    inherited the benefit of a doubt.
That's your birthright.
                    A man may have a million bucks
in his pigskin billfold,
                    but you're still ten steps ahead.
I'd say, Do Mama
                    & Granny have the benefit,
too? He'd grin & say,
                    Hell, yeah! But, son,
you're already miles ahead.
                    Then we'd each take a spoonful
of our homemade peach ice cream.
                    Granny would appear big
as an Oklahoma sunset in the doorway
                    with her hands on her hips,
& say, Gus, please don't
                    teach that boy your craziness.
A new day is around
                    the corner. I could see my mother
getting smaller. My father
                    was somewhere on his touring bus
outside Orlando or skirting
                    Las Vegas, humming a new song
under his breath as they rounded
                    a curve. Sometimes
she cried herself to sleep

　　　　　　　　　or drank small bottles of rum,
& then we'd chew Juicy Fruit
　　　　　　　　　till I could see the man
in the moon sitting on the windowsill.
　　　　　　　　　　　　　Grandpa would whisper,
I don't care what your Granny says.
　　　　　　　　　　　The benefit of a half doubt
is worth more than gold in the bank,
　　　　　　　　　　　more than rubies & diamonds
stolen out of the eye sockets
　　　　　　　　　of some Egyptian sun god
hidden in a cashbox in the Florida Keys.

◎

I went off to college
                    two years after my father & Jack McKinda
bought the Chimera Club,
                    before he sold his touring bus.
I went off to college
                    with colors & songs
inside my head. Lies
                    & stories that lasted for hours.
For days. Weeks. Months.
                    Years. For a lifetime
in no time. Like I said before,
                    if you start me talking
I'll tell everything I know.
                    Back then, my whole brain
was a swarm. A hemorrhage
                    of words & colors. I wanted everything
at once. I wanted to see
                    & hear everything. I wanted to be
everywhere. Climb every rock
                    & cross every river under the devil's
last sunset. I was good at math.
                    Good at biology. I loved
Proust & Lorca. Trig
                    & folly. But nothing made me happy.
So, after two years,
                    I found myself back home, my face
pressed against the night
                    windows, daydreaming centaurs
& tomorrows filled with lovely girls.

◎

When my draft notice arrived
                          I was twenty, with apparitions
of Vietnam on the six o'clock news
                          clouding my head. That afternoon
I brought the unopened envelope
                          down here to the Chimera Club
where my father pulled beers
                          & told stories of his touring days
before rock 'n' roll
                          cut the floor from underneath him.
I placed the envelope on the bar.
                          He poured me a big shot of cognac.
That was my first drink
                          in his bar. A field of ghosts
& a lifetime ago.
                          I downed my shot of cognac.
He opened the envelope
                          & said, Drinks are on the house,
everybody. That's all he said.
                          My mother was another story.
I never heard her curse before,
                          but she said, Those bastards
sent you their goddamn death letter,
                          & now I can't have another drink
till they bring you home. Roberta
                          said, You go upstairs
& start packing your clothes.
                          You're my boy,
& you're going to Canada.
                          I'm not going to stand here
& let them bring you back dead

in a steel box. My forefathers
ran off to Canada,
& now you're on your way too. That night,
my mother pulled a chair
to a bedroom window,
to where she could stare out
toward the white mailbox
beside the green driveway.
Since Daddy hadn't gone
to World War Two,
he was now gung ho
& didn't want white feathers
to fall from the sky
onto his doorsteps.

◎

Before our banana-shaped chopper
                    landed at Cam Ranh Bay
the oldest silence fell
                    over everyone. The South China Sea
played with a few round
                    fishing boats, as white sand
ferried away the beginning
                    & end. The night black
silk, beyond minds on firepower
                    & deadly prayers. Smoke
huddled between hills where
                    fifty-gallon drums of shit burned.
A few gunships circled upwards
                    like great bubble-headed
dragonflies in the green
                    distance. We tried not to look
into each other's eyes,
                    afraid of our lives staring back
at us. We would soon belong
                    to rats eating C-rations
in our bunkers, as water bugs
                    fattened on darkness. Roaches
in the ears & noses of the living
                    & the dead. If greenness
were woven into the weather,
                    into jackfruit & lotus
blooms, how could there be
                    death in my mouth?
If we could see the future,
                    some of us were on stretchers

with bottles of lifewater
                    swaying from side to side
as angry feet ran on earth
                    & somewhere else among those
lost planets & dead stars.

◎

At first, I felt as if I were falling
                              in love with the wives, daughters,
& sisters of the dead NVA
                              & Vietcong. Their whispers
sighed through the water
                              reeds & rice shoots, calling
to the monkeys, the tigers,
                              & the two-step vipers,
as if summoning the land
                              to march its greenness against us.
Sometimes, I'd sit on the edge
                              of a grassy gully
at dusk, watching ant-soldiers
                              run back & forth,
carrying their wounded
                              from the dragonfly copters,
& my fucking heart
                              would leap up & burst open
in that air made of loneliness & nitrate.

◎

The reason I drag
                    my left leg this way,
I took a sniper's bullet
                        outside Da Nang a week before
my short-timer's calendar
                            turned blue. My platoon
was crossing a rice paddy
                        at dusk, the day's end
white with salt & the weight
                            of green sky, a silent
singing in the wild throat
                        of everything there,
& then mist rose as if from
                        the deep belly of night hunger
& the birds stopped, before
                            monkeys crawled inside
the brain & eleven kinds of fear
                            clustered around the thing
worn to a bone. It were as if
                        the sniper had been born
for that moment, for nothing else
                            on earth—without mother
or father, without heart or history,
                            the sun a purplish bruise
that moment we went back
                        walking on our hands.
Where did the bamboo
                    grove spring up from?
I was running for it,
                    but I couldn't move. Our machine gun
answered the trees

& questioned the evening star.
Three voices were calling
                        Medic God Momma.
Sergeant Dixon had warned
                              the greenhorn with butter bars
not to stand so close to the radio
                                operator, & now he was holding
his guts in his hands. Lord,
                        Father of Jesus & bastards—
they were moving toward us.
                        Why aren't we returning fire?
My mind was working,
                        but my tongue was dumb as a clapper
in a midnight bell. My blue eyes
                              were water-level
with the rice shoots.
                        Two boy-faced Vietcong
wheeled their curved blades
                              as if to harvest melons
or some nameless crop to save
                              their souls. Where was I?
I kept asking till moonlight
                              glinted off a raised scythe,
& I could hear the first choppers
                              lifting off the ground
like great birds of prey floating
                              toward the dead. The dead
running toward me as I ran.
                        The VC were trying to outrun
the definition of God,
                        boy-faced in my head still today.
I shoved Carson's body
                        off the .30 caliber,

& all that blue-black
                    metal & naked hush began to do
its death dance again.
                    They ran with three heads,
& the marsh reeds
                    & elephant grass began to bloom
as if begging
          to be forgiven. I don't know
if I should say
          what I never said before—gut wounds
& head wounds, blood
                ran into the last rays
of sunlight, mixing with night
                        a sky heavy as the darkness
inside the first human grave.
                        The rice plants trembled
with the dying platoon, the slush
                        turning redder. I could hear
the swoosh of the chopper blades
                        low over the low jackfruit
trees, a door gunner's gaze remembered
                        through reefer smoke,
the great hum & hangnail of light
                        against an eternity of blue.
I wasn't on earth because death
                    was all over me, from head
to feet, first word to last song . . .

◎

If the President wishes to know
                              what's happening, why
hate festers like locust swarm,
                              he should walk in, sit down,
order a Bloody Mary,
                              & I'll tell him
how the mouth entangles
                              brain stem & genitalia.
Bamboozled by too much light
                              to see, dumbfounded
down to seed in our core,
                              only if we were half as brave
as we'd like others to believe—
                              we stand snaggletoothed,
grinning into an unhealed abyss.
                              Sometimes I sit here, perched
on this stool like John Howard
                              Griffin, knowing what I know,
afraid my face betrays
                              as I listen to salt poured
into the wounds. Because
                              my skin's white as ten mouths
cut into alabaster,
                              they believe I am them,
but I want to say,
                              When you can breathe for me
you can tell me who to love
                              & what to think.
I have felt my flesh & blood
                              used, the usury of honey
some unnameable grief weighs

                              against each petal & crushed bud
under a wanderer's bootheel.
                      I look at them, as if
they fashioned themselves from spit
                              & clay, sperm & ghost
egg—a bone key to unlock the gates.

◎

I can't press a fingernail
                    into the President's name
till a jay cries from its tower
                    of green leaves, a fortress
of springtime branches,
                    because he didn't go to Nam.
Sometimes I wish that Silver Star
                    never came out of its velvet-
lined box. They can melt it down
                    for a boy's tin whistle
at a crosswalk, a lucky charm
                    for a guy burning his draft card
in Canada or Sweden. I know men
                    who did more than I dreamt,
& only received a smudge of blood
                    on bronze because of black
or brown skin, shortchanged by a pen.
                    Sometimes I can't stop
thinking of Oliver, a paratrooper,
                    just eighteen, who threw himself
on a VC's hand grenade
                    to save his squad, who turned into mist,
into something less than a ghost
                    of memory. For weeks,
for months, I could taste him in the dust.
                    Do you know how it feels
to have your tongue shaped
                    from a dead man's name?
Suppose that grenade
                    hadn't fallen like jackfruit
from a scarred branch,

          & Oliver walked in here
tonight, took a seat beside
          Nancy, & they began to talk.
I have played the scene
          over & over in my head:
the grenade, the three hundred years
          of silence, the air swollen
with only our voices. The others,
          where are they now, what
are they saying about Oliver?
          If he had fathered children
would song or lament bloom
          in their dark mouths? Today,
what kind of man would he be,
          is that sound still traveling
out into space, among the stars?

◎

I did what I did. To see

                    friends turn into ghosts

among the reeds, to do

                    deeds that packed the heart

with brine & saltpeter

                    was to sing like a bone

for dust. All the questions

                    were backed up

inside my brain. Questions

                    I didn't know I had—

as if I had stopped

                    at the bloody breach—

the stopgap between

                    animal & human being.

I did what I did.

                    I called the Vietnamese

gooks & dinks

                    so I could kill them. But one night

I had to bash in the skull

                    of a dying GI.

I was the squad leader,

                    but I didn't order

PFC MacHenry to do

                    what I couldn't do.

Or Private Ortega.

                    I used the butt

of my M16,

                    & stars bled on the grass.

Was the soldier black?

                    Was he white?

I can only say
         I did what I did because
he sounded like a pigeon
                tied to a hunter's stool,
cooing with his eyes sewn shut.

◎

When I returned, I hitchhiked
                                a year with my dog
Bullet. She was the only one
                        who hadn't come to me
as a stranger, wagging her tail
                                as if I'd gone around the block
for an hour. I left my mother
                                waving in the doorway, my father
drunk in the den. With guitar
                                & rucksack, we slept in bindweed
& kudzu, apple orchards
                        & ball fields, beneath trestles
& in voluptuous, borrowed beds
                                in one-horse towns, flophouses,
& parks in big cities,
                        wild songs & flowers
in my wild hair. I thumbed
                        the pages of dog-eared
Articles of War, a ghost
                        of Nam still in the clothes
I wore. I was thankful
                        for the Big Dipper & the night
owl in the oaks, thankful
                        Bullet hadn't barked or growled
at me that morning, as she'd done
                                so many times before
when I brought home
                        the slow perfume of women
on my clothes & hands.

◎

This damn rain
                  makes me think of
a monsoon with horses
                          running inside it, forcing the grass
& trees to bow, firing
                  bullets of wet light
straight down
              to the underworld.
I tell you, on a day
                  like today, Good Samaritans stay
hidden. Two years ago,
                    one night like this rainy night,
some joker in a blue suit,
                    a white shirt & yellow tie,
said to me, Empty
              the till, & I said to him,
Mister, please
             don't make me hock
my hands again
              to the devil. I was at least
three feet from my .38,
                  but I said what I said
anyway. He surprised me
                    when he dropped his peashooter
& ran out of here,
              & then I looked over
toward the cash register
                  & saw my old man
standing there. It seems,
              for company,

he'd brought along
                    the soldiers—the two friends
I lost in the jungles.
                    I hope you don't
feel like this weather
                    is holding you prisoner.
But I tell you, I'm happy
                    to have you here,
someone to talk to,
                    because on a night like tonight
there's an army of shadows
                    unearthing Kingdom Come
& rallying the dead.

◎

You won't believe this,
                    but I have a twin sister.
Her name's Wagadu,
                    & she lives in Berkeley,
California. At least, that's where
                         I saw her in the flesh,
walking into the Blue Nile,
                    as if she'd floated up
out of four other shades of grace
                         & infection, several lifetimes
away from her Soninike village.
                         I'd known her years before
I ever saw her, this albino
                    from somewhere out of a naked
wail song held down inside
                    the body, as if my deepest thoughts
turned into blood. I first
                    glimpsed her coming out of Cody's
where I lived that summer
                    between the stacks, thumbing pages
that redeemed & betrayed.
                         Someone called her Sila, & somebody else
said Agada. She'd always be
                    on the other side of the street
like the hint of a shadow
                    passing through white paper,
endless pages of an epic
                    illusion. She was there
& wasn't there. Dierra
                    & Ganna are the other names
she's known by.

◎

Okay, let's talk about loneliness.

                        Once, a long time ago,
I had me a woman.

             Her kisses were blues.
The words she spoke

                had a little echo inside them
because her tongue was gold,

                   & one wanted to steal songs
out of her mouth. My hands

                dreamt of the Bronze Age
because her breasts were gold.

                  Her hips were bullion
& her cunt was 24k.

               Her hair was so golden
it was jet-black at high noon.

                  Yes, once upon a time,
I had me a woman

             made of solid gold, but one day
a flit of gold-colored desire

                caught my foolish eye
& I broke the vow

          that followed a vein
down to the underworld.

◎

It took five years
             for me to phone
my mother & father.
                   I was in Red Rocks,
Colorado, with a woman
                   called Gypsy. She rode
an apple-green chopped-down
                   bike, & worked as a stripper
in Las Vegas. Once a month,
                   she'd ride over
& return after a few days.
                   I worked in a soup kitchen
in Colorado Springs,
                   when I wasn't at the Red Door
talking to soldiers headed for Nam.
                   I wondered if they could see
the ghosts sitting beside me. Free love
                   & Acapulco gold, Janis
& Jimi, Creedence Clearwater Revival
                   & the Grateful Dead,
Otis Redding & Marvin Gaye—
                   the Garden of the Gods.
The mountains stopped
                   & pushed me up against
the blue sky. But one day,
                   I found myself in a phone booth
calling home, to be wounded
                   by my mother's first words:
Son, last night
             the doctors gave Roberta
her last code blue.

◎

Old Blue Eyes. *Don't*
                *get around much*
*anymore. Don't get around*
                    *much anymore.* Do you remember
Joyce, who used to work
                    day shift here, a black woman
with red hair & freckles?
                        Remember? Well, one August
afternoon I came in for swing
                    & said, Joyce, what's wrong,
girl? There was silence,
                & then she began to cry.
You see, her hands—
                she has the most beautiful hands,
& they were shaking
                like darkness trying to hold
too much light.
                I said to myself, Ah,
hell, what did I say?
                    Sinatra was on the jukebox.
Old Man Fred's double shot
                    of Cutty Sark sat here
on the bar, waiting for him.
                        Joyce said, That lowdown bastard
is gone, & now the damn worms
                    are on their way to him.
Thank you, Sweet Jesus.
                    Then slowly, she told me the story
about Old Man Fred,
                how he'd punch the same
Sinatra tune three times

on the jukebox weekdays
between four-thirty & five,
how he always left a two-dollar tip.
She said, I feel guilty.
Guilty? I said. He had to be
at least seventy-five.
She took out a handkerchief
& blew her nose,
& then faced me again & said,
Old Man Fred confessed
when he found out he had cancer.
I feel I shouldn't know
what I know,
how he & his two friends
killed a black teenager
because he was dating a white girl,
how they beat his head in
with a tire iron & shoved his body
into the Tallahatchie,
& how he proposed that Saturday
to his girlfriend, Shirley.
Is this now my story to tell?
All I know is this: the boy
in the Tallahatchie can't speak
& Joyce is now somewhere
in Seattle. Old Man Fred
is dust on the gooseberries
boys eat along the roadside.

◎

When my father was dying
                    he begged my mother
to forgive him, & she'd say,
                    Forgive you for what,
darling? He'd shake his head,
                    with a fat tear sliding down
the corner of his nose,
                    & he'd say, Honey,
I don't know.
            Between June & August,
two crows sat in the dogwood
                    outside their bedroom window,
& when their calling subsided,
                    my mother would say, Darling,
do you have the strength
            to forgive yourself?
Her question hung
            in the air—an old-old silence,
as if forgiveness
            was a luminous alchemy.
He'd look at me & say,
                    Son, would you please
remind your mother,
                    would you tell her what I did?
Big hero, with your Silver Star,
                    flesh of my flesh, your eyes
say you know all my secrets
                    along this long road,
& the least a son can do
            is to help his father
nail his shadow to a pink dogwood.

◎

Sometimes I feel broken. My arms
                     a boy's, daydreaming
baseball & horseshoes. My legs
                    with weights tied to them.
One part of me feels unlived,
                   & another feels almost used up,
licked clean by too many desires
                 good for one man. Sometimes
it seems I've been everywhere—
                  Adam's Bridge, Les
Eyzies, Nicobar, Swan, Zadar,
                 A to Z, & then again
sometimes it feels as if I hadn't
                 been broken in yet,
depending on how daybreak falls
                 into a bedroom window.
I've bartended here
          at the Chimera Club
for twenty-some-odd years,
             but I've also worked
as a tool-&-die man in Detroit,
              a dogcatcher in Manitou Springs,
a blackjack dealer in Biloxi,
             a dishwasher at The Cosmic Onion
East Side of the Big Apple,
             a gang boss in Galveston,
& I smelled nothing but death
             for over a year on a floating rig
factory off the coast of Alaska.

                        Yes, friend, there are seven
or eight jobs I'm too damn
                        ashamed to say I've done,
with the salt of love in my eyes.

◎

Do you know this tune,
                        do you know who's playing
tenor? Listen. Listen.
                        You have to know
who this is, the only one
                        who would cock his horn
& talk with the angels
                        & demons of the deep,
trembling night. Listen.
                        Here's another thing about war:
any man who can plead
                        through a hunk of brass
this way, could never kill
                        another man. You can't
talk to God & kill a man
                        in the same breath. No
way. He loved this tune:
                        "Almost Like Being in Love."
Yes. Listen. That sound
                        is his, driven by his blood.
It isn't for anyone to steal,
                        or drip down to nothing
but a whimper in the dark.
                        I won't let them put rap
or hip-hop on this jukebox,
                        or any damn race records
either. It has to be truer
                        than gold. Listen. Listen.
Do you hear what I hear,
                        how he follows the sound
out of the horn, to the edge?

                    Where do you think
he's taken us, back to skeletons
                              chained on the seafloor,
or is he beside Lady Day
                    standing in buttery sunlight?
You can almost turn
                    any corner, can almost
beg to be forgiven
                    for each carbine, shell, or grenade
your hands lingered on.

◎

Iraq? Well, as I said before:
                    If you start me talking,
I'll tell everything I know,
                    & now I'll say this:
Please, America,
                    let's forget the old warfare
of skin color & hair.
                    I can see a gutted palace in Hue,
dust devils rising from the ashes
                    of Operation Phoenix. Gods
fighting other gods.
                    The looting & pillage
of museums in Baghdad—
                    the shattering of a porcelain pig
with a ball-peen hammer.
                    Looters running with engraved images
& figures, statues, icons, & cuneiforms
                    stained with the blood
& shit of war. Some are messengers
                    of the dead, trying to hide
treasures from the infidels,
                    as if we're the last horde
of barbarians storming the gates.
                    Others, of course,
are filling orders for this blue jug
                    of Sumerian clay shaped & fired
on the bank of the Euphrates,
                    or that statue lying like a dead child
in a heap of rubble,
                    the shadow of a desert
ram burned into it.

◎

The blond poster girl
    of this war, I can't
remember her name. Amy,
      Melissa, Jennifer, Jessica?
Like a captivity story
    that circles back, corralled
inside the brain—Indian braves
      riding ponies into the sunset
with a white woman.
    But when this poster girl
refused any false honors
    & medals, she disappeared
from the headlines & magazine covers.
      She could still hear
the old Iraqi woman
    whispering into her ear
as the doctors worked
    in their bloodstained room,
& maybe a question
    hummed inside her head:
Why is our enemy
    always dark-skinned,
always surrendering an arm
    & a leg for a tooth,
a child for an eye?

◎

Ah. Abu Ghraib.
                Guantánamo. Lord,
if the dead could show us
                     where the secret graves are
we'd walk with bowed heads
                  along the Mason-Dixon Line
till we're in a dusty prison yard
                  in Angola or Waycross,
or we're near the Perfume River
                  or outside Ramadi. You see,
the maps & grids flow together
                  till light equals darkness:
an eye, a nose, an ear, a mouth
                  telling a forbidden story,
saying, Sir, here's the skin
                  growing over a wound,
& this is flesh interrogating a stone.

◎

Now, I say this,
              this song that isn't in hock
to my father's tongue.
                  Words that leap out of my mouth,
pulling me to the past,
                 pulling me into myself
till I can almost feel
                what that football hero
felt when friendly fire
                shook open the sky
over his head, the moment
                  he knew he didn't die
the way they said he died.
                  This pale gauze of words.
The gauze for hidden wounds
                  unraveled this rainy night.
This last call for the road.

◎

Forgive the brightly colored
                    viper on the footpath,
guarding a forgotten shrine.
                    Forgive the tiger
dumbstruck beneath its own rainbow.
                              Forgive the spotted bitch
eating her litter underneath the house.
                         Forgive the boar
hiding in October's red leaves.
                    Forgive the stormy century
of crows calling to death. Forgive
                    the one who conjures a god
out of spit & clay
               so she may seek redemption.
Forgive the elephant's memory.
                         Forgive the saw vine
& the thorn bird's litany.
                    Forgive the schizoid
gatekeeper, his logbook's
                    perfect excuse. Forgive
the crocodile's swiftness.
                    Forgive the pheromones
& the idea of life on Mars.
                    Forgive the heat lightning
& the powder keg. Forgive the raccoon's
                         sleight of hand beside
the river. Forgive the mooncalf
                    & doubt's caul-baby. Forgive
my father's larcenous tongue.

Forgive my mother's intoxicated
lullaby. Forgive my sixth sense.
Forgive my heart & penis,
but don't forgive my hands.

Nancy Crampton

YUSEF KOMUNYAKAA
## WARHORSES

Yusef Komunyakaa's twelve books of poetry include *Taboo* (FSG, 2004), *Talking Dirty to the Gods* (FSG, 2000), and *Neon Vernacular: New and Selected Poems*, for which he received the Pulitzer Prize.